Wild Animal
TRACKERS

Rob Waring, *Series Editor*

HEINLE
CENGAGE Learn

T0052337

Australia • Brazil • Japan • Korea • Mexico • Singapore • Spain • United Kingdom • United States

Words to Know

This story is set in South Africa. It happens in the Karoo [kəru] National Park. A **national park** is a special area where nature is protected.

A **Wild Animals in Africa.** Read the sentences and label the pictures with the underlined words.

A herd is a large group of animals.

Africa has many wild animals like elephants, zebras, and giraffes.

People often find wild animal tracks, or footprints, in Africa.

1. _____

2. _____

3. _____

4. _____

5. _____

B Conservation Technology. Read the paragraph and notice the underlined words. Then answer the questions.

African Bushmen can track, or follow, animals very well. They can learn many things by tracking animals. However, the Bushmen can't always tell other people what they know. They don't always speak the same language. This story is about a conservationist named Louis Liebenberg (libənbɜrg). He is helping to protect Africa's wild animals. He has developed a new kind of technology for getting information about the animals. It's a method that doesn't depend on spoken language. It's called 'The Cyber Tracker.'

1. What does '**language**' mean? _____
2. What does '**conservationist**' mean? _____
3. What does '**technology**' mean? _____

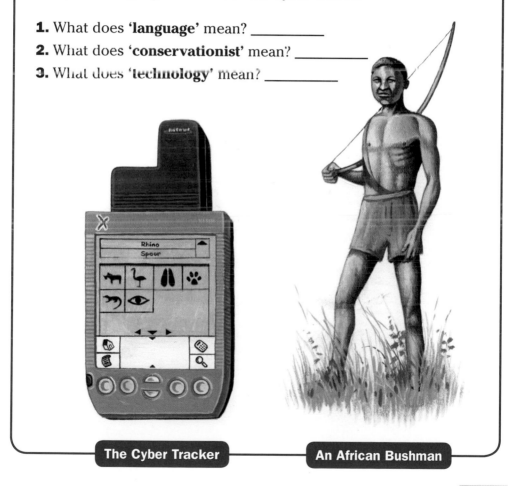

The Cyber Tracker

An African Bushman

In some parts of Africa, there are still big herds of wild animals like zebras, elephants, and giraffes. But today many of these wild animals are in danger because people are taking the land that the animals need.

It's a big problem that worries many conservationists. Conservationists are people who protect wildlife and nature. And some of these people are now leading a fight to save these animals.

🎧 CD 3, Track 09

Louis Liebenberg is one of the conservationists who is trying to save the wildlife of Africa. He feels that having good information about the animals is very important for success. "The most important thing is to try and get an understanding of what's happening out there," he says.

Liebenberg reports that people need to know more about animals. He says that people need to understand what happens to plants and animals over time. Are they increasing or decreasing in numbers? What plants are the animals eating?

Summarize

What does Liebenberg mean?

1. Summarize paragraph 1 in one sentence.

2. Summarize paragraph 2 in one sentence.

African Bushmen may be able to help conservationists to answer these questions. For hundreds of years, Bushmen have understood the ways of animals like zebras and giraffes. They're very good wild animal trackers. The Bushmen know what the animals eat. They know where the animals go. They even know where they sleep.

However, there is a problem. The Bushmen don't always speak the same language as the conservationists. This can cause problems when they work together, and communicating information is sometimes difficult. This is where new ideas and new technology can help.

This is where the Cyber Tracker comes in. The Cyber Tracker is an **invention** [1] created by Louis Liebenberg. Liebenberg has brought the invention to the Karoo National Park in South Africa. He hopes that together, the Cyber Tracker and the Bushmen can help protect the animals. He thinks it's a perfect match of modern technology and old knowledge. But what is the Cyber Tracker?

Liebenberg explains that it's a small computer that helps collect information about animals. It uses pictures, called 'icons,' instead of words to record information. This way, the Bushmen can record what they see even without words. They don't have to read or speak the same language as Liebenberg or others. According to Liebenberg, the Cyber Tracker can collect very detailed and **complicated** [2] information very quickly.

---

[1] **invention:** a new machine that has never been made before
[2] **complicated:** difficult; with many parts

However, that's not the only thing the Cyber Tracker can do. The small computer also contains a **global positioning device**.[3] Each time a Bushman sees something interesting about an animal or plant, he pushes a **button**.[4] The Cyber Tracker records exactly where the man is in the world. That way, even if the man can't read or write, he can record what he sees and where. But how does the Cyber Tracker record information?

---

[3] **global positioning device (GPD):** a machine that tracks where things are on Earth
[4] **button:** a small key on a machine

button

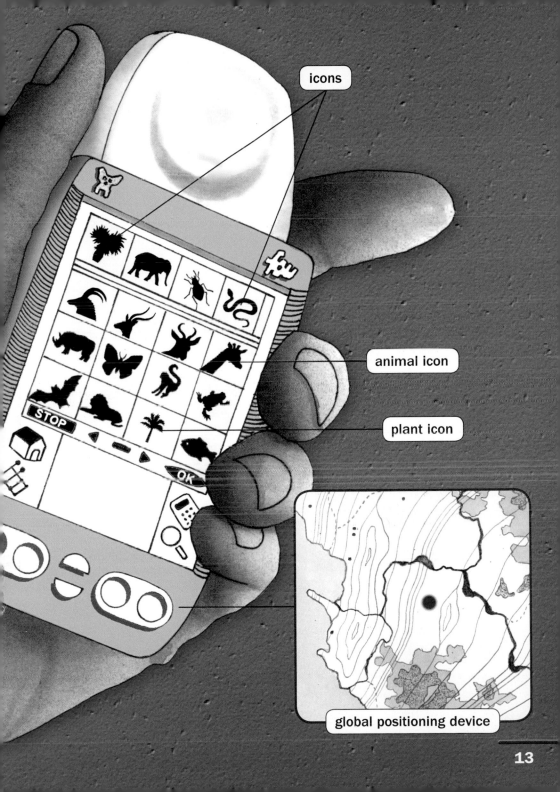

icons

animal icon

plant icon

global positioning device

STOP

OK

Liebenberg explains that the Cyber Tracker uses icons to communicate. There are pictures for drinking, walking, fighting, sleeping, eating, and other things. With the Cyber Tracker, the user can report whether an animal is sick or dead, too. The Bushman also can record other meanings by pushing different buttons. With this option, they can name about 50 different plants. This becomes very useful when the Bushmen want to record what the animals are eating.

However, Liebenberg adds that it's not just about the technology. According to him, the human factor is also very important. Liebenberg says that a big part of using the Cyber Tracker is the Bushman's ability to record the information. He must be able to understand and correctly report everything he sees. The combination of machine and man seems to work very well.

When the trackers return to their base, they connect the Cyber Tracker to a personal computer. Then, Liebenberg looks at the data and uses it to make **maps**. [5] These maps show where the animal herds are. They also give information about what the animals are eating, and indicate facts about their health. Liebenberg can get a lot of detailed information about a lot of wild animals.

---

[5]**map:** a detailed picture of a specific area

The Cyber Tracker project started five years ago. At first, the idea was to help a few animals in danger. Because of this, the invention was used only in certain situations. Nowadays, the Cyber Tracker is used much more often. More and more people have started using the Cyber Tracker in other African parks. They have also started using it with many different kinds of animals.

Recently, Liebenberg has even put the Cyber Tracker **software**[6] on the Internet. Now many conservationists around the world can get the software. They have started adding the technology to their conservation programs. The future of the Cyber Tracker looks good. Soon, it may be able to help in the conservation of wild animals everywhere.

---

[6]**software:** computer program

Scan for Information

Scan page 18 to find the information.

1. When did the Cyber Tracker project start?

2. What was it first used for?

3. Where can people get the software now?

4. What may the Cyber Tracker soon be able to do?

After You Read

1. Each of the following is happening to the animals in Africa EXCEPT:
   A. Conservationists are helping them.
   B. The land they need is being taken.
   C. There are fewer and fewer of them.
   D. They are in danger from the Cyber Tracker.

2. In paragraph 2 on page 4, the phrase 'leading a fight' is closest in meaning to:
   A. working hard
   B. arguing
   C. disagreeing
   D. protecting

3. The best heading for page 7 is:
   A. Animals Eat Plants and Increase
   B. Conservationist Wants to Know More
   C. Liebenberg Wants to Know Exact Number
   D. Conservationist Takes Space from Animals

4. Bushmen know _____ about animals.
   A. very
   B. nothing
   C. a lot
   D. too

5. In paragraph 1 on page 8, who is 'they' in 'they sleep'?
   A. animals
   B. bushmen
   C. conservationists
   D. Liebenberg's group

6. How does the Cyber Tracker make communication easy?
   A. People can see where the Bushmen are.
   B. The invention uses pictures for language.
   C. The software can identify about 50 plants.
   D. Conservationists can write down information.

7. The purpose of the Cyber Tracker is to:
   A. help with communication
   B. collect information about animals
   C. track animals
   D. all of the above

8. What initials are used for 'global positioning device'?
   A. GPS
   B. GPD
   C. GSP
   D. GDD

9. In the first sentence in paragraph 2 on page 15, 'it' refers to:
   A. technology
   B. global positioning device
   C. recording information
   D. pushing buttons

10. The Cyber Tracker helps to get _____ about animals and plants.
   A. maps
   B. computers
   C. information
   D. trackers

11. The writer probably thinks that:
   A. Every student should have the Cyber Tracker.
   B. Technology is making conservation easier.
   C. Louis Liebenberg is a famous software maker.
   D. The Cyber Tracker is difficult for conservationists.

12. According to page 18, which of the following will NOT happen in the future?
   A. The Cyber Tracker will be added to other conservation programs.
   B. The Cyber Tracker will be able to help animals everywhere.
   C. Conservationists won't be able to get the Cyber Tracker software.
   D. All of the above.

DAILY News

GLOBAL POSITIONING DEVICES BECOME INCREASINGLY COMMON

The invention of the satellite over fifty years ago opened the way for the Global Positioning System (GPS). GPS uses a series of satellites to provide exact information about the location, or position, of certain objects. There are currently 24 GPS satellites in use. There are also three additional satellites if one of the 24 stops working. Originally, only the United States government was able to use the system. Today, however, people everywhere can use GPS technology for free. This is making Global Positioning Devices (GPDs) much more common.

GPS uses a series of satellites.

screen

buttons

Most GPDs are very small.

A GPD is usually a small machine with a screen and several buttons on the front. They are often about the size of a cell phone. First, a GPD sends information to several satellites. This information tells the system where the user is; however, it must reach at least three satellites to work correctly. Next, GPS measures the GPD's exact distance from each satellite. It then sends this information back to the GPD. Finally, the GPD uses special software to change this information into a map with marks on it.

GPDs are like having a map that follows you wherever you go. They allow the user to see where he or she is at any moment. People can use the information to track where they have been or to plan where they want to go. Fishermen have discovered how useful GPDs can be when they are out on the open water. People lost in the woods can now find their way home. Many of today's new cars include GPDs. Drivers choose an end point and the GPD shows them the best way to get there. Some people are even placing GPDs on other people. They want to know where the person is at all times. The possible applications for GPDs are endless. Who knows where they'll show up next?

CD 3, Track 10

Word Count: 330
Time: _____

Vocabulary List

animal track (2)
button (12, 13, 15)
complicated (11)
conservationist (3, 4, 7, 8, 9, 18)
elephant (2, 4)
giraffe (2, 4, 8)
global positioning device (GPD) (12, 13)
herd (2, 4, 16)
invention (11, 18)
language (3, 8, 11)
map (16)
software (18, 19)
technology (3, 8, 11, 15, 18)
zebra (2, 4, 8)